Left to their Devices...
What's Left?

Left to Their Devices... What's Left?

Poems and Prayers for Spiritual Parents
Doing Their Best in a Digital World
(and leaving God the rest)

Gloria DeGaetano
author, *Parenting Well in a Media Age*

ISBN: 978-1-4497-5336-8 (sc)
ISBN: 978-1-4497-5337-5 (e)

WestBow Press books may be ordered through booksellers or by contacting:

WestBow Press
A Division of Thomas Nelson
1663 Liberty Drive
Bloomington, IN 47403
www.westbowpress.com
1-(866) 928-1240

Library of Congress Control Number: 2012908906

Printed in the United States of America

WestBow Press rev. date: 7/20/2012

To spiritual parents doing their best
and leaving God the rest.

Contents

Introduction   ix

Poems and Prayers   1

    Left to Their Devices   3

    Today's Friendly Reminder   4

    You'll Get Used To It   6

    Centered in the Holy Within   8

    We Watch Grown Ups Play Dress-Up   10

    Use My (Your, Our) Imagination   11

    On Amazement's Edge   13

    Empty Me   14

    Prologue   15

    Spirit, Hear My Longing   16

    Denying Divinity   18

    Prayer for Parental Presence   19

    Post-Personal World   20

    Some Crazy Robot   20

    Cookie-Cutter Kids   21

    Mean Stupidity   21

    Ask the Parent of a Bully   22

    Prayer for All Children   24

    We Love Our Children in Two Worlds   25

    Dear God, Give Me Wisdom's View   26

    You Don't Own My Children   28

    Help Me Refuse Peripheral Parenthood   29

Space Talks   31

Make Our Home Your Sacred Space   32

A Connected World   33

Keep My Higher Self in Your Keeping   34

Left to Our Own Devices   35

Your Whispers, My Actions   36

The Children of Tomorrow   37

Blessings for This Day   38

Parting Words   39

About the Author   41

Introduction

"Love is the essential reality and our purpose on earth. To be consciously aware of it…is the meaning of life. Meaning does not lie in things. Meaning lies in us." ~ Marianne Williamson

I appreciate this quote by Marianne Williamson because:

1. Parental love is indeed, our "essential reality." Yet often in the midst of the stresses of modern-day life, we easily lose sight of this "conscious awareness"—not through any fault of our own. But because, that's the nature of the times we live in. When you think about it, moms and dads have to parent side-by-side a popular culture that delivers messages, images, attitudes, and priorities instantaneously to children, often in opposition to what we want and what we know is best for them. Children today live in a culture that parents don't intentionally create.

2. Popular culture promotes meaning in things and status—in what lies outside ourselves. This quote reminds me "meaning lies in us." Parents. Period. I find this a grounding affirmation for living in spiritual integrity alongside an overarching culture we cannot directly control.

Since 1987 I have helped parents proactively meet the seemingly endless challenges that media and screen technologies bring to families. What I have realized over the years is that as technology changes, it requires us to grow new ways to parent to ensure our children thrive. We can't stick our heads in the sand and ignore the issues. And we can't throw our hands up in the air and give up, either. Yet, if truth be told, that's what many parents feel like doing. Certainly understandable.

In these pages I have tried to capture the various dilemmas described by the moms and dads I work with—spiritual parents like you who are doing their best, but often feel overwhelmed, exhausted, distressed, even fearful, while trying to figure out how to navigate popular culture, media, and the new digital landscape.

The strong statements and sentiments in *Poems and Prayers* are not intended to cause guilt or unease, although they may do both. Rather, consider them a collective soul expression that may resonate with you—maybe even inspire you when making decisions about media/digital issues in your household.

One way to read this book is as a meditation—a quiet time for you to pause and ponder. As you "go inward," I invite you to contemplate your role as a spiritual parent.

- Do spiritual parents have a unique responsibility for helping other parents understand (and do something about) the negative consequences of over-use and inappropriate use of screen technologies in childhood and adolescence?

- Should spiritual parents be expected to make wise choices for their children—even if it means their friends ostracize and ridicule them? Even if it means *your* peers ostracize and ridicule *you*?

- Should spiritual parents be exceptionally courageous to confront (and do something about) the corporate culture's hold on children and teens?

- Should we anticipate that spiritual parents will lead society away from the suffering of screen addiction toward life-affirming uses of screen machines for positive connection and meaningful education?

- Should we encourage spiritual parents to usher in a new world of "Wisdom first…then technology?"

And…if spiritual parents don't step up to this work, who will?

Surely, not schools. Increasingly becoming mere managers of technology-based learning, many schools can't understand why they fail. Perhaps they have forgotten that devices can't teach? Only teachers can teach. Computers, i-pads, laptops, and cyber-spaces are tools for learning. Amazing tools—but not effective—and probably damaging—if they replace teachers—who alone can respond to children with guidance, teaching discernment, restraint, and use of screen technologies for intentional purposes.

Academic researchers who study the harmful effects of over-use and misuse of screen technologies can't do much to help parents, either. Their hands are tied because the commercialized culture invests in silencing them. Even though their research is meticulous and convincing (there is a greater statistically significant correlation, for instance, between watching violent media and becoming aggressive than there is a correlation between lung cancer and smoking), these well-intentioned researchers can't get the attention of the airwaves to influence parenting decisions around media and digital technologies on any large scale.

Traditional media outlets often obscure what's best for our kids. Here is one poignant example: The American

Academy of Pediatrics (AAP) strongly urges parents to keep children from birth through age two completely screen-free. Now, you may know this. But if you do, you are among the 6% of American parents who somehow have managed to receive this important message in the midst of much opposing, muddled information. When I was on *The Today Show* discussing Baby Einstein videos, my position was in alignment with the AAP's. But the professor I was "debating" had the opposite view. How could that be? Well, she was under contract with a large, powerful company that promoted a similar video series for babies and toddlers. Many influential academics are actually spokespeople for the corporations who own the media that enable their visibility.

Obviously politicians aren't equipped to deal effectively with this issue when they can't make positive changes about fundamental issues like poverty or health care. So that leaves parents with a conscience. Parents like you.

Our society is at a crucial crossroads. We can't leave our kids to their devices because if we do, they don't belong to us anymore. They belong to a commodified culture dominated by global conglomerates. This is not a human culture: it is a marketplace. And as we know, marketplaces cannot rear children in God's image. This book aims to:

Gently remind moms and dads to use their own devices—gifts of Spirit and human skills and talents—to parent well in our digital world, knowing that if we don't, we risk losing our children to screen addiction and to unfulfilled lives.

Please join me and other spiritual parents spreading this important message. I wish you courage and unflinching confidence. I pray with you for both.

Gloria DeGaetano
Bellevue, WA

Poems and Prayers

Left to Their Devices

The gadgets seduce our young in a modern-day siren song, promising power, but delivering addiction.

Children imprisoned in a screen-world, can't remember what they never experienced—God's close world of warm breezes touching apple cheeks, soggy soil squeezed through pudgy fingers, the wonder of dandelion fluff blown sky-high by a single breath.

Distracted from essential earth, how will children know real human connections tested in trial and renewed in embrace?

Preoccupied by the trivial, do they hear their deep Selves starving for the authentic?

Attention distorted, spirits mangled, will crushed, still…we leave them to their devices.

Left to their devices, childhood becomes a barren terrain and adolescence a consumer carnival.

Left to their devices children see empty reflections in the mirror of a social network, desperately seeking themselves in others.

Left to their devices, we abandon children to predatory practices and call it capitalistic competition.

Left to their devices, we strangle parental power to insure our kids belong to the crowd.

Left to their devices, children miss what they want most and don't even know it passed.

Today's Friendly Reminder

Dear God, today's friendly reminder: This is my child we are talking about. This isn't some white lily in a field with a 3-week life span. This is my beloved, most precious child—born innocent, pure, born like You, (You said it Yourself.) So really…This is *our* child You need to protect, enlighten, and guide in this crazy World of the Gadget.

But then again, You do know we are not talking about lilies in a field, don't You? You want me to trust that if you take care of flowers, well piece of cake for You to take care of the children…But right now, at this time on earth, excuse me, but I just don't get it. I need to see/understand much more to trust You.

These are babies, only 90 days (or less) out of heaven with devices as playthings. Perhaps i-phone rattles signify the death-rattle of our culture?

Where are the adults leading the charge? Has spiritual backbone disintegrated?

Don't you agree with me Dear Lord that babies, toddlers kept busy by and taught by machines is a form of child-soul abuse? You certainly know how fragile those little brains/minds/hearts are, how impressionable—so how in God's name (*sorry!*) in this Day of Information can adults not understand digital dangers for the very young?

How do so many adults—even those who claim to know and love You—give up Your majestic natural world so easily? They dive into their devices and never look up again. Now they have their babies doing the same.

Dear God, this is beyond my scope of understanding.

Please grant me the necessary patience and non-judgment. You can see both are very hard for me…And, at the same time, I need courage to remain in my integrity to do what I think is best for my child. What I know in my heart is best for my child.

If we are created in Your image, dear Lord, did you mean for us to become extensions of machines? Or did you mean for us to manage the machines for higher purpose? To stay human and use the machines wisely? I think so, but how?

Please guide me, and all the parents who are working so hard to figure this out. I need clarity because right now I'm frightened for my child's future and insecure about my own. I feel like I walk everyday on a trembling, gaping crack in the ground that will widen unexpectedly and down I and my family will go. Never to be seen again. No one will know. No one will care. Family extinct.

I pray for strong footing on Your solid ground. I pray for the peace that comes with that. I pray for a path to guide me and mostly I pray You protect my child.

You know it takes a lot more to grow a child than it does a lily. I'm trusting You on this one. So please remember on your busiest days, especially, this is not a lily we're talking about, this is my precious, amazing, child—a child made in Your image. You said so Yourself.

You'll Get Used To It

"You'll get used to it." That's what my friend told me when I protested the new changes on Facebook.

"But I don't want to get used to Timeline," I complained, knowing full well that I would get used to it, even though in the moment, I hated the fact Facebook was dictating what I needed to do, even though in the moment, I abhorred the idea of yet more time and investment to figure it out—again—still, I knew I would get used to it. Why?

I got used to e-mailing, then I got used to tweeting and posting. Initially shy about sharing photos on-line, I got used to that, too.

I got used to connecting instantly with friends around the globe; I got used to speed and multi-tasking. I got used to using my i-phone and i-pad. I got used to having these devices close. I got used to giving and receiving immediate replies.

I also recall how I got used to watching reality TV. At first, the strong emotional displays embarrassed me, but over time, tears shed by bachelorettes stopped fazing me. I am less moved by unrequited love and less shocked by voyeuristic love than I used to be, because, well, I got used to it.

I think of kids who get used to virtual killing as child's play, now acceptable forms of delight and satisfaction. I knew a time when that was considered abnormal, even psychopathic—but they got used to it—and evidently so did society.

I think of tots who don't play outside anymore or who go out to dinner with their parents and watch a movie while their family talks around them. Family conversation going the way of the dinosaur and everyone getting used to it.

If we adapt so easily to both the harmless and the harmful, can we distinguish between them?

And is this the way from here on out?

Technology gives us something new. We're not sure about it, but hey, we tell ourselves, "You'll get used to it."

And we do.

Centered in the Holy Within

Dear Holy Within, you anchor me and keep me wholly within a spiritual framework of parental decision-making. You are Center. Please center me in what's really important today as I struggle to stand firm in the midst of continual change.

Novelties distract me. Their cacophony erodes my resolve. I know "the new and improved" are intentionally created by marketers, strangely reminiscent of carnival barkers, who desperately need people to buy. Their insistence wears me down, Lord. Usually I'm torn in so many directions I feel like a spinning top on the way to total collapse—especially when my children nag me for the new toys, gadgets, apps, games, etc. when I'm trying to get dinner on the table or otherwise preoccupied. Then, when they make a point: If all their friends have it, shouldn't they have it too? It starts making sense to me.

Forgive my weak accommodating. Forgive my yielding to the pressures. In these confused family times, the easy way seems like the only way. You know I'm only trying to do what is best for my children. I want them to be happy. That's what I'm thinking of when I make a rash decision. Yes, in the short-term everyone's satiated and preoccupied. In the long-term, though, there is always the hunger for more. And then the cycle begins once again, driving me nuts.

I really don't want to give in. I really want to stay true to what I believe.

Please guide me in my weakest moments. Protect me from

the gilded idols of our age that relentlessly seek to replace Your priorities in my heart. Protect me from a quick parenting decision I will regret later. Reassure me that just because a new type of technology is "out there," doesn't mean I have to bring it "in here" into my home.

Dear Holy Within, You anchor me and keep me wholly within a spiritual framework of parental decision-making. You are Center. Please center me in what's really important today so I feel less reactionary and much more responsive.

Centered in the Holy Within, I am at peace, knowing my parenting decisions arise from thoughtful considerations.

Centered in the Holy Within, I respect myself and better appreciate my dedication to my children.

Centered in the Holy Within, I look at the world through loving eyes and listen with an open heart.

Centered in the Holy Within, I experience calm and confidence despite swirling chaos.

Centered in the Holy Within, I am wholly the parent I want to be. And I hope…I am the parent You want me to be.

We Watch Grown Ups Play Dress-Up

We watch grown-ups play dress-up and call them stars,

While we worship their psychosis and along the way,

Young imaginations starve.

Forsaking make-believe, hollow-eyed little people mimic adults in offices, fixed to screen-machines.

The resplendent passes them by. No notice.

No time for costumes, plot, or dialogue—no possibility hunting.

After all, you can't conjure what could be without a will to innovate or a burning desire to create.

That ember left long ago.

We got it all wrong. Paying millions to adults for romps in the imaginal world while the little people here in this world enter someone's else world, not knowing how to escape.

Use My (Your, Our) Imagination

Dear Lord, help me use my (Your, our) imagination in growing my child to use (his/her Your) imagination.

Images of life, deep caring, and compassion no longer easily surround and embrace my child…I have to do that in our home, our family sanctuary. It's daunting, and seemingly futile, given what I hear and see each day. Help me provide the counter images of life, love, respect, harmony with nature, positive people, generosity, kindness—all the images I would want in my child's own imagination.

Help me to remember in the midst of busy family daily living—to pause and make imagination possible for my child. Plenty of pieces, fragments, color, sensory delights—placed before my child like waiting altars offered to You for Your blessings.

Bless my child with gifts of Your Spirit so my child discovers Your life energy in her imaginative meanderings.

Help me be the mind-full parent I strive to be.

Please give me the will on days when I am dragging, so physically tired I can hardly see straight, please bring me new stamina to take a moment to engage my child in imaginative play. This takes more Mom-energy than I have some days. I need You then more than ever. I need You to be my back-up, my tap on shoulder that says, "Yes, this is all worth the tremendous effort you are putting in right now. Hang on. You will be delighted at the results as your child grows."

In my head, I do know that a child with an imagination is never a bored child, never a boring adult. We just have to tell that to my body when I'm exhausted.

Three tiny prayers I will say today...

Dear Lord, grant me the energy to make a special effort to nurture my child's imagination.

May Your beauty ignite my child's authentic innovation.

May Your inspiration ignite my true originality.

Amen.

On Amazement's Edge

A bored child sits on amazement's edge, teetering toward wonder. With glimpses of potential still foggy, cruel uncertainty requires a faith yet to be discovered.

A bored child fidgets, sighs, nags, fidgets some more, craving amusement but yearning for recognition of Self.

A bored child thinks quick relief from the tyranny of nothing to do brings the same result as finding what is wanted to do.

Brooding, resisting inner-world feasts, a bored child has one foot in the fertile void, but doesn't know it. That next step may need your nurturing nudge.

There are dark spaces to light and musty corners to clear out—plenty of choices to sift through—all must be discovered alone, probably uncomfortably.

A bored child insists you make it better, easier, quicker. Resist the pleadings (please), turn away from the whining; extinguish your urge to fill the emptiness.

A bored child sits on amazement's edge, teetering toward wonder, waiting for you to shift the lens of attention, longing for you to say:

"It's OK to be bored, honey. Here…these are your special inside glasses. Put them on. Close your eyes. Look inside. Sit quietly. Take your time. Sit. Wait until you find it…you will invent it from inside of you. I know that. And when you do, you will never be the same…ever…again."

Empty Me

Dear Lord, empty me of distrust, doubt, and fear. Fill me with trust, faith, and, courage. Empty me of my personal wishes and replace them with Your special purposes.

Empty me of what I think I know and pour into me what You know I need to know.

Help me to sit quietly in that dark void without conjuring up worries or making up new problems. Keep my mind-chattering to a minimum as I work to let the day's frantic activities gradually drain off like snow slowly melting into a mountain stream.

May You carry me in that stream to where I need to go as I lie afloat on Your grace, not moving, listening, taking into my heart: "Be still and know I am God."

In Your stillness may I find ripeness and renewal—a new me unfolding and filling the empty space to greet tomorrow's challenges and uncertainties.

Dear Lord, empty me of distrust, doubt, and fear. Fill me with trust, faith, and, courage. Empty me of my personal wishes and replace them with Your special purposes.

Empty me of what I think I know and pour into me what You know I need to know. Thank You.

Prologue

The Web shimmers in the sunlight. Majestic marvel.

From afar one notices the glimmering, connected intricacies —too many possibilities. So we jump into its allure. We bathe in its steady light. What a huge ever-present world. Keeping us always on call; ever ready to respond. Let's make sure to respond rapidly, nicely—after all this is about being and staying informed, available, cool—and of course, marketable.

The latest app ushers in more new worlds, learnings, functions, choices. The latest must-have gadget makes our hearts sing. How entangled through a day of sunshine do we want to be? But are we even noticing the sunshine?

We surf, adapt, and adapt, and surf. Click here then here then here then here…Spinning those threads so quickly now, we can't tell we're holding our breath more often, or crouching for hours paying homage to a machine.

Hey, That's us trapped in the web's sticky ropes. And yet (unbelievably!) we are in denial. We actually think we have something meaningful to say by parroting the hive mind.

Human autonomy extinguished in the numbness of enslavement, we can't see or feel our entanglement.

We giggle in the face of extinction.

Unfortunately, the fly thinks it's the spider. And this is merely the prologue.

———— ∞ ————

Spirit, Hear My Longing

Spirit, hear my longing…

My child needs to belong to me, our family, our personal community. The impersonal community of the Web can't do for my child what we can. I know this, yet, I can't find a way for the personal to outwit the impersonal.

Spirit, here's the battle I face each day: When's he's here, with us, his personal community, he wants to be there—in the Web. When he's there, I doubt if he gives us a second thought, a mind glance. The Web encompasses him and he loves it. I can't get him away from it.

Social-Personal and Social-Web are different experiences. I want my child to have as many social-personal as he does social-web experiences. And ideally he would be able to take the best of both types of experiences and learn to be authentic in relationships, courageous in intimacy, fearless in love.

Spirit, hear my longing. Guide me to know what to do to parent from my highest Self. Enlighten me to the right words to say, the proper tone to engage him to listen to reason. We must balance his life—and mine.

I don't know if he knows he belongs now more to the on-line community than to his family. I am not sure he sees our relevance any more. This sadness crushes me.

Watching my child get sucked in like this and so angry when asked to come back to us—well, there are no words to describe how this disturbs me.

$\mathcal{S}$pirit, hear my longing…

My child wants to belong to me, our family, our community, personal and present. Please grace me with the wisdom to know how to bring him back to us. Amen.

Denying Divinity

A fragile soul has to be propped up,

Like a floppy puppet on a narrow ledge,

Has to care what others think,

Has to pay more attention to what's without than to what's within.

A fragile soul allows the occupation of corporate colonization and believes it's necessary nurturance.

A fragile soul gets easily confused.

Actually denying its divinity, a fragile soul can't know its strength nor claim its authentic power.

This denial is not voluntary or even conscious.

It's a natural outcome when strong souls forget their heavenly heritage and allow machines to tell them who they are.

Prayer for Parental Presence

Holy Spirit, please shed your generous grace on me for calm, inner, careful quiet. I desire to be fully present to my child with mind, heart, and soul, with the whole of me. Help me to discover Your soothing Presence within. Remind me to breathe deeply when listening to my child, looking in those big eyes, window of the child-soul, so my parental presence speaks loudly, "Yes." "I am here for you." "I am with you." "I love you so."

Holy Spirit, may Your warm, renewing Light germinate within me a lasting peace—a peace so profound, it's contagious and my entire family catches it! With this peace I can make every conversation with my child a sacred moment. With this peace, I become present. And...I open up space for You to be present between us—parent and child.

With Your generous Grace, the distractions and daily disturbances no longer agitate. Your loving Presence fortifies my resolve to stay present.

With my loving intention visible, viscerally felt, my child grows in full presence to the Divinity within. Your Presence encircles our presence with each other, creating endless sacred moments for both parent and child.

May Your blessing of Parental Presence remain alive in me throughout this day. Amen.

Post-Personal World

Announcing…The post-personal world, the time of the reptile resurgence since we left our frontal lobes on the shelf somewhere back in 1995, right in the middle of the decade of the brain, and we forgot entirely that thinking and feeling are related and that we need people to do both in order to stay people.

Some Crazy Robot

Some crazy robot woke me up in the middle of the night and told me,

"I am now your children. You must take care of me."

I said, "You're crazy, my children are asleep in their beds dreaming of playing in wide open fields of tall yellow grass and violet flowers.

He said, "No, they're not. Follow me."

We marched into their rooms. Empty. Empty beds with messy quilts and covers—no bodies, no souls, no dreams. I screamed. Please let me wake up—but this was no nightmare.

The crazy robot made up the empty beds precisely, right down to the military corners and tight sheets.

Then he left the room.

Cookie-Cutter Kids

Cookie-Cutter Kids look out their windows and can't see the beauty, instead they see themselves. Or replicas of themselves. Does it matter?

Collectively no longer individuals, they think the same, act the same, imagine the same, want the same, talk the same, and eventually will parent the same.

Cookie-Cutter Kids look out their windows and can't see the beauty, instead they see themselves. Or replicas of themselves. Does it matter?

———— ❦ ————

Mean Stupidity

Mean stupidity frightens, baffles, and frustrates—mostly it hurts.

It hurts to see the young heart/mind trashed, thrown aside forgotten on a dung-heap of superficial sham.

It hurts to see dull 13-year-old eyes spark only for the grotesque.

It hurts to know that elder wisdom becomes totally useless when techno-glam fills personal voids.

It hurts to watch toddlers caged by screen machines, limiting their capacity to ever walk away.

It hurts—a lot—that mean stupidity rules because smart adults cower.

———— ❦ ————

Ask the Parent of a Bully

Ask the mother of a bully if she first gazed at her precious newborn swaddled in white and felt all creamy softness and saw all the glowing newness and said to herself, "Yes, you will make a mean, cruel child one day, I just know it."

Ask the father of a bully if he built forts with his toddler and taught him to bat the ball across wild weeds and ran after him over and over as he darted for the fence, keeping him safe from the traffic, and then rolled on the dirt with him, loving to feel his warm, chubby hands around his neck, why don't you ask him if ever wondered in these moments, "You will punch and bruise and name call and want for friends once you are in junior high."

Ask the parents of a bully if they sat in church for 11 years of Sundays with their son or daughter and watched the young eyes (even glistening now and then) absorb the sermon's lessons of love and compassion, ask them, did they ever on one Sunday or more think to themselves, "You will not live these lessons while at school. You will ignore, forget, or dismiss all these Sundays—totally perplexing us."

Ask the single mom of a bully if in her wildest dreams while observing the tender moments between the siblings for years of weekday chores and brisk Saturdays raking leaves that she could ever imagine her eldest would grow up mean, laughing at others' misfortunes, shutting out hers and others' love?

Ask the single father of a bully who raced home from work, too rung out to do anything but with enormous effort oversaw the homework, practiced the multiplication tables until they blurred on the page, explained arithmetic to calculus with saintly patience, ask him if during these years of shoulder-to-shoulder mentoring, he once considered that unkindness would grow to drown the math skills; that his own kindness couldn't stop the decay?

Parents do not set out to create bullies. Bullies are shaped by the unmet needs often hidden from parents in a society that scorns difference and loathes originality.

Parents give their best with what they know at the time. Sometimes that works and is enough. But sometimes, as baffling as it sounds, their love, good intentions, and constant work aren't enough—through no fault of their own—through no shortcoming—no lack of will, desire or inability to love—sometimes as incredible as this sounds in this Day Of Information—sometimes,

Parents do not know what children really need. Real developmental needs, when not fulfilled at the appropriate times, often result later in a form of emotional or physical violence to self or others.

Not intending to raise a bully is not the same as intending to not raise a bully.

Prayer for All Children

Dear Lord, I read the other day that 50% of kids are bullied at school. If this statistic is correct, that means all our children have become either a victim or a bully. How has this happened?

I pray to You...

Grace all children with confidence and gentleness. May they be so sure of themselves they naturally are kind to others.

Help all children know how to choose caring friends.

Guide them toward harmony and mutual respect, released of cruelty, one-upmanship, defensiveness.

May all children be healed from the inside hurts, no longer needing to send their pain to others through words or deeds.

Lead them to the right adults who will hear them, affirm them and free them.

May all children, from tots to teens, know and appreciate their magnificence and in so doing, radiate Your magnificence to others.

May all children feel safe in the knowledge of Your love.

May all children be safe in the promise of Your protection.

Amen.

We Love Our Children in Two Worlds

We love our children in two worlds.

The screens, phones, games, the Web, the fabric of cyber-connect form a world our children inhabit, but parents don't create.

Moms and dads make breakfast, dinner in a hurry, drive kids nearly everywhere so they won't be left behind, work hard to carve out time for snuggles, quality connection, meaningful nuance. This daily world built minute-by-minute by parents doing their best, that's the world where children grow to know who they are and can strive to be all that they can become.

Parents nudge, coax, invite, demand, tell, urge, plead for children to stay in the world of the human. To enjoy this world as much as they enjoy the other world.

The screens, phones, games, the Web, the fabric of cyber-connect form a world our children inhabit, but parents don't create, confusing the human journey, confounding parents, reducing their role to Managers of the Machines.

We love our children in two worlds.

Each world calls in different ways; each pulls in different directions. Each wants our children's attention and intention.

We love our children in two worlds.

And pray the best world wins.

Dear God,
Give Me Wisdom's View

I see Wisdom as the most massive eagle ever, big enough to hold planet earth in her formidable wings. She soars above us all. She sees all sides of any divide, knowing what's best in any matter. She can swoop down in a nano-second to disturb complacency and deepen dialogue, enlightening speaker and listener alike.

Wisdom makes everything better without judging the worst. Wisdom forgives the failed. Wisdom transforms struggles into surprises. Wisdom comforts with the knowledge that yes, you made the wise choice from the mountains of choices before you.

Dear God, give me Wisdom's View to see my child's world from the larger frame—to open my mind to the positive possibilities. To know that you have given us immense knowledge technologically speaking and now it is time for Wisdom to rule over the World of the Gadget. I want a piece of that Wisdom to hold onto each and every day as I talk with my child and work to help her become a wise user of all things high tech, as I make sure she has time to know the ground of her being in Your holy natural world.

It will take Wisdom's view to succeed as a parent in today's world—a world of two worlds constantly colliding. Tech-tools aren't divine, they are just devices. My child must know human divinity and divine humanness more than how to navigate social media or win at the latest Wi game.

Dear God, give me Wisdom's View and the gentle understanding that I am doing my best and leaving You, Loving Creator, the rest.

You Don't Own My Children

I have news for you Corporate Conglomerates, Greedy Billionaires—you don't own my children—and you never will.

My children belong to all that is green, growing and alive—not to your death traps, your cold calculations.

My children belong to the warm heavens, to all space with endless possibility, to caring human hearts that work diligently, determined every day to keep you at bay.

My children belong to every pine needle that ever existed, to all the air that was ever exhaled, to the dust of ancestor bones.

My children belong to sound and light, music, art, science, thought, and dance—to originality, innovation, to promise and purpose. My children belong to God.

I have news for you Corporate Conglomerates, Greedy Billionaires—you don't own my children—and you never will.

I am making sure you keep your grubby hands off, your filth far away, your destruction to yourself. My children, as precious as Life itself, God's image in miniature now, full-bloom if I succeed, deserve to live free, protected by my love.

I have news for you Corporate Conglomerates, Greedy Billionaires—you don't own my children—and you never will.

———&&&———

Help Me Refuse Peripheral Parenthood

Oh God, stop me from becoming the peripheral parent—You know, the one who can't say no to texting at the dinner table (or even at church!), or who acquiesces to every whim and logo-infested wear for the sake of a temporary peace.

Please don't let my guilt debilitate my discernment and please—keep me involved. It's so tempting to stay on the sidelines because what parent likes daily hassles, endless debates, and draining confrontations?

Oh God, stop me from becoming the peripheral parent who shies away from playing the video games first before buying, who worries if I'm upsetting my child when saying "No" to "games" that in reality are murder rehearsals.

Help me stay the un-cool parent, who is really me, the one whose heart does know that hours on end in front of a screen (every day of childhood and adolescence) isn't a good thing. Screen-machines can't build souls. It's that simple. Yet, so complex. Vigilance exhausts me and that's when I'd like You to step in.

The earth needs my child and my child needs time on it. Help me remember this when screams for the screen machine mean rage against going outside on a clear, blue, crisp day. I must force earth-experience…and I can only do so with Your help.

Help me stay in that uncomfortable, disturbing place of the unpopular culture, the parent culture, the personal culture—what I truly believe in and know to be best for my child.

Dear God, I long for a society of human parents influencing their children deeply, and in turn, youth respecting age and real knowledge. Parents being worthy of respect.

As a spiritual parent I can lead the way to this New World—this world of Parent Culture—our brightest beginnings and fondest of hopes. Yet…

I can't do this if I'm a peripheral parent. You know that.

———∞∞———

Space Talks

"What surrounds the child, teaches the child," the great John Dewey once wrote.

Meet Mr./Ms. Space, the invisible air, yet influential persona who mentions this or that without regard to child-level appropriateness, who carries messages instantly to defenseless brains, never knowing (or caring) their effect.

Meet Mr./Ms. Space, weightless yet filled with meaning, unable to comprehend the enormity of its influence—clueless consciousness with viper precision.

Meet Mr./Ms. Space, no persona or texture, yet palpable, real, steeping children in images and voices human parents wouldn't dare choose.

Meet Mr./Ms. Space, a close ghost, making sure the distant stranger enters into our children's spirits completely, irrevocably.

Make Our Home
Your Sacred Space

Dear God, make our home Your sacred space, a quiet haven for hearing about each other, being with each other, for listening deeply and responding wisely.

Infuse the air in each room with your Divine Perfume, a mystical mist proclaiming our ordination into the Sacrament of Family. Duly anointed, may we remember to create an air of mutual respect, treading softly, with kindness, open to Your love to soften and guide us.

Make our home Your sacred space, a tender atmosphere preciously packaged for deep encounters of the most intimate kind. May the space around us absorb this love and feed it back to us as we move together in our daily preoccupations.

Dear God, may the space that speaks to my children in our home be Your sacred space. May we keep the digital disturbances controlled enough for abundant connections with each other—in laughter, questions, dialogue, delight— in fun and energy and lively understanding.

May Your sacred space in our home give us the blessed arena to speak to each other when we want to, to hug when so inclined, to fully focus on each other as the norm. May Your sacred space in our home propel us toward each other and not let anything—no device, gadget, or machine come between us. May Your sacred space be our home. And may our home be Your sacred space. Amen.

A Connected World

A connected world doesn't mean we have to, or must disconnect from our Self.

That Self bathes integrity to purify intent,

And yearns for a relevant voice in a connected world.

A connected world doesn't mean we have to, or must disconnect from our Self.

That Self sets limits to build capacities,

And discards the irrelevant for what's necessary in a connected world.

A connected world doesn't mean we have to, or must disconnect from our Self.

That Self cites the essential to fortify the mundane,

And invites us to share our collective wisdom with each individual.

A connected world doesn't mean we have to, or must disconnect from our Self.

In fact, a connected world mandates strong connection to Self.

After all, that Self is our path to life; our way to God.

Keep My Higher Self in Your Keeping

Dear Lord,

Five Good Reasons to Keep my Higher Self in Your Keeping:

1. My Higher Self in Your keeping knows humility, seeks Your will, and discerns better.

2. My Higher Self in Your keeping perseveres without complaint and acts decisively, knowing that High-Self choices hold a good track record.

3. In Your keeping my Higher Self is a blossom who must burst forth, always conscious that the impetus to bloom germinates from Your Creative Source—not from her.

4. In Your keeping my Higher Self operates from the central intelligence of Your loving womb, continually nourished by Your sustaining Grace.

5. My Higher Self in Your Keeping has the best chances of side stepping ego's confusion and diminishment.

Thank You for keeping my Higher Self in Your keeping.

Left to Our Own Devices

Left to our own devices, we muster forgotten courage, speak confidence to our wisdom, and raise heaven (instead of hell).

With our own devices, we become guiding adults again, no longer conspirator co-dependents in our kids' addictions.

We shed timid skin and grow the recognizable thick skin of the parent who does whatever it lovingly takes to keep children intellectually open, emotionally healthy, spiritually sound, reachable. And then miraculously...

Fueled by fierce love, graced with character, strength and courage by the Divine, our own devices become divine devices.

We live meaning outside of those gadgets.

Adorably alive, our children see that.

We parent fully human.

Our children become that.

Your Whispers, My Actions

What you quietly reveal to me, Dear Lord, please don't let me ignore. Help me to face and overcome the difficulties of parenting in this digital world by trusting Your whispers to become my actions.

Usually, though, I can barely hear you in the midst of all the daily noise and my loud complaints about much of the everyday grind. The hustle of each day preoccupies me so much that frankly on many days, I'm just too worn out to hear you.

Speak up! Wouldn't that be nice? Voice of God interrupts MTV for a special message to parents…hardly. Yet, with the screen blaring, I have to make sure I have enough quiet moments to hear You. Most days, I find this difficult to do.

Dear Lord, I'd like to be a parent with some solid inner space. I'd like to be mindful with an empty mind; and thoughtful without a thought. I know I can listen to You best that way. Hearing Your marching orders and doing them aren't the same thing. You usually urge me right out of my comfort zone into the seemingly impossible place that only becomes possible with Your grace. Help me remember that.

Please guide me to trust Your whispers to become my actions. Help me stay open to all potential within me and around me. There's a lot to do beyond my family for my family and for all families.

Dear Lord, help me to trust Your whispers to become my actions. Thank You.

The Children of Tomorrow

The children of tomorrow live in our marrow, breath in our cells, sing in our laughter.

Their health depends on our choices—small and large. We expand or limit them by what we do or don't do today.

The children of tomorrow listen to our stories for fragments of unfulfilled dreams; for guidance out of desolation and confusion.

Their intelligence depends upon our choices—small and large. We enhance or diminish their mental powers by what and how we think today.

The children of tomorrow read our words and wonder, question, learn—develop reasons for living or excuses for quitting.

Their will depends upon our choices—small and large. We inspire or dismay their stirrings by what we envision and accomplish today.

The children of tomorrow may have big warm open hearts or cold blood in their selfish veins. We're not sure yet.

Their capacity for love depends upon our choices—small and large. We build loving souls by intentional selflessness and joyous giving today.

The children of tomorrow sit comfortably in space waiting for their chance, watching us take ours. Their fulfillment depends upon our choices—small and large. We bring them a life worth living, by living a worthy life today.

Blessings for This Day

Dear God,

Grant me patience so I am fully present today.

Grant me prudence so I can make good decisions today.

Grant me peace to bring forth the best of me today.

Dear Lord, during the gift of this day shine your blessings on my family.

May we grow in love for each other and for You.

May we make time for each other and for You.

And may all parents remember that what we do today changes the world for our children as well as for the children of tomorrow.

May today's children respect us and may tomorrow's children be grateful to us. Amen.

Parting Words

"How do I know when I do my best?"

For years I was haunted by this question. Growing up my Mom would always say to us kids, "Do your best and leave God the rest." But she told us this, if we got A's or failed; if we made the team or if we didn't. The outcome proved inconsequential—if we did our best that was all that mattered.

But how do I *know* when I do my best?

Later life taught me that I don't ever know exactly. I may be able to know approximately, but not for sure. I can assess my intention, commitment, willingness, and level of participation. I can determine how I embrace responsibility. I can observe my procrastination, reluctance, noting what worked to breakthrough. Ultimately, though I must humanly conclude, "Given my time, limitations, my current knowledge and understanding, the extent of my resources, OK, I guess I did my best."

So it's always a qualified best (at best)...perhaps that's because God wants to fill in where we fall short.

In this digital world, let's all do our best...and leave God the rest...and then, who knows...?

May these wise words of Helen Keller inspire us onward:

"When we do the best we can,
we never know what miracle is wrought in our life
or in the life of another."
~ Helen Keller

About the Author

Gloria DeGaetano, internationally-acclaimed educator and author, directs Parent Coach International™, a global community she founded that brings parents and professionals in family support together for dialogue and decisions about what's best for kids. Gloria originated the parent coaching profession, developing Parent Coach Certification®, a year-long, graduate-level training program credentialing teachers, counselors, and social workers as certified parent coaches. Assisting parents and educators with media-related challenges since 1987, Gloria has written many articles and several books including *Television and the Lives of Our Children* and *Stop Teaching Our Kids to Kill: A Call to Action Against TV, Movie, and Video Game Violence* (with Lt. Col. Dave Grossman). Her book *Parenting Well in a Media Age,* won the 2007 i-Parenting Media Award for excellence.

For moms and dads who wish to take time to renew their lives and re-adjust their family's relationship with media and digital devices, Gloria offers *Retreats for Spiritual Parents.*

For more information, please see
www.LeftToOurDevices.com.